NE'ER-DO-WELL KNITS

MAKE A LITTLE TROUBLE

HUNTER HAMMERSEN

D1602431

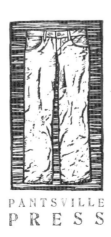

PANTSVILLE
PRESS

Charts created with StitchMastery Knitting Chart Editor.

ISBN: 978-0-9849982-3-4

First Printing, 2013

Printed in China

Pantsville Press
Cleveland, Ohio
www.pantsvillepress.com

Contents

Introduction 1

Patterns

   Miscreant 2

   Scoundrel 4

   Ruffian 10

   Vandal 14

   Brigand 18

   Saboteur 22

Tips & Tricks 27

Thanks 28

Resources 28

INTRODUCTION

You can't be good all the time. It would be exhausting. Worse yet, it would be boring. I firmly believe we all need to make a little trouble from time to time. But just because you're up to no good doesn't mean you don't want to look great.

Whether you're taking a walk on the wrong side of the tracks, persuading that lock to click open, clambering in through a conveniently open window, or just stirring up mischief, these patterns will make sure you're doing it in style. And if pulling out your knitting happens to make you look innocent and unassuming to any members of the local constabulary who might come strolling by in the middle of your adventures—well, that's just an added bonus!

MISCREANT

These addictive little cuffs are as close to instant gratification as knitting gets. A clever eyelet edging transitions into a tidy slipped stitch ribbing. You'll be done (and itching to start the next one) before you know it.

SCOUNDREL

These socks are unabashedly, unapologetically complex. An intricate mirrored cable, a detailed heel flap, and a sculpted toe all demand your attention. But the reward for all your careful work is a gorgeous sock that's well worth the effort.

RUFFIAN

This pair of coordinating hats offers two variations on a theme. One technique (an unreasonably entertaining dropped stitch) leads to two totally different looks. You only ever use one yarn per row, so these hats are a perfect way to get comfortable using two yarns in one project.

VANDAL

These socks are surprisingly easy, despite their undeniably impressive appearance. The twisted columns and deeply embossed leaves carry right through to the heel and toe for a pleasingly polished look.

BRIGAND

These sculpted mitts are simple yet charming. A stately cable and a delicate thumb gusset combine to produce a mitt that is both beautifully fitted and eminently comfortable.

SABOTEUR

These socks are downright girly. The delicate lace on the leg tapers to a sharp point on the foot. The result is a beautiful, feminine sock that is just as much fun to knit as it is to wear.

MISCREANT

Shown in: Astrid by Space Cadet Creations in a one-of-a-kind color. Made with the 88 stitch cast on with about 75 yards of yarn.

Gauge and Sizing: 6 stitches in 1 inch in ribbing as shown on rows 5 and 6 of Main Chart. Fits a wrist of 5 [5.75, 6.5, 7.25, 8] inches. Measure at the widest part of the forearm that you want the mitt to cover

Main Chart

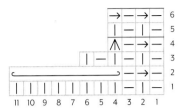

Cast on: Cast on 77 [88, 99, 110, 121] stitches. Place marker and join for working in the round.

Frill: Work rows 1-4 of the Main Chart. 28 [32, 36, 40, 44] stitches remain.

Wrist: Repeat rows 5-6 of the Main Chart until wrist reaches desired length

Finishing: Cast off loosely. Weave in ends. Block if desired.

| Knit

— Purl

→ Slip as if to purl with yarn in back

⋀ Centered double knit decrease

⌐━━━━━━━━⌐ Eyelet

Note: The red lines on the chart indicate repeated rows.

Centered double decrease: Slip 2 together at the same time as if to knit 2 together. Knit 1. Pass the slipped stitches over.

Eyelet: Knit 1 and put it back on the left needle. Slip the next 7 stitches (one at a time) over this stitch and off the needle. Yarn over twice (you'll treat each of these loops as a seperate stitch when you work the next row). Knit 1 (it's the same stitch you knit at the beginning of the eyelet).

SCOUNDREL

SHOWN IN: Merino DK by String Theory in the color Carina. Made in size Small with about 375 yards of yarn.

GAUGE AND SIZING: 7 stitches in 1 inch in stockinette. Fits a foot or leg of about 8.5 [9.5] inches.

NOTES: To make the socks mirror each other, you must start and stop following the Main Chart at different points. Pay close attention to the instructions.

CAST ON: 60 [68] stitches. Place marker and join for working in the round.

CUFF AND LEG: For sock 1, work the Main Chart (starting at row 1) until sock reaches desired height. Stop after completing row 10 or 20. Note where you stop. For sock 2, work the Main Chart (starting at row 11) until sock reaches desired height. Stop after completing row 10 or 20. Sock 1 and sock 2 will stop at opposite points. Note where you stop.

HEEL FLAP: The heel flap is worked over stitches 32-60 [38-68] of the leg, plus 2 extra stitches that are added as you start the heel flap. It uses a total of 31 [33] stitches. The way you add the extra stitches differs depending on where you stop the leg. Be sure to follow the appropriate directions.

In either case, odd rows are wrong-side rows (worked with the inside of the sock facing you, following the wrong-side notations in the stitch key, and reading the chart from left to right). Even rows are right-side rows (worked with the outside of the sock facing you, following the right-side notations in the stitch key, and reading the chart from right to left).

If you stop the leg after row 10, you will create 2 extra stitches the first time you finish working row 1 of the appropriate Heel Chart. To do this, work a double increase on the final stitch of row 1 as shown in the appropriate Heel Chart.

Work row 1 of the appropriate Heel Chart once. Work rows 2-5 of the appropriate Heel Chart 8 [9] times or until heel flap reaches desired length. Stop after completing row 4 of the appropriate Heel Chart.

If you stop the leg after row 20, you will create 2 extra stitches before you begin working the heel flap. To do this, work to the end of the last row of the leg shown in the Main Chart. Before turning to begin the heel flap, pick up the purl bump at the beginning of the previous round (it's stitch 1 of that round). Purl into the front and back of this stitch. You've now got 2 extra stitches on your needle. Work the appropriate Heel Chart 8 [9] times or until heel flap reaches desired length. Stop after completing row 4 of the appropriate Heel Chart.

HEEL TURN: Odd rows are wrong-side rows (worked with the inside of the sock facing you). Even rows are right-side rows (worked with the outside of the sock facing you). Turn at the end of each row.

Row 1 (WS): Sl1, p17 [17], p2tog, p1.
Row 2 (RS): Sl1, k6 [4], ssk, k1.
Row 3 (WS): Sl1, p to 1 stitch before gap, p2tog, p1.
Row 4 (RS): Sl1, knit to 1 stitch before gap, ssk, k1.

Work rows 3 and 4 until 19 [19] stitches remain.

GUSSET AND FOOT: Pick up and knit 1 stitch in each of the slipped stitches along the side of the heel flap, place first marker. Work across the top of the foot following the next row of the Main Chart (either row 11 or row 1) for 30 [34] stitches, p the 31st [35th-37th] stitch[es], place second marker. Pick up and knit 1 stitch in each of the slipped stitches along the other side of the heel flap, k9. The round now begins in the middle of the bottom of the foot.

Decrease round: K until 3 stitches remain before first marker, k2tog, k1. Work across the top of the foot following the next row of the Main Chart for 30 [34] stitches, p the 31st [35th-37th] stitch[es]. K1, ssk, k to end of round. 2 stitches decreased.

Non-decrease round: K to first marker. Work across the top of the foot following the next row of the Main Chart for 30 [34] stitches, p the 31st [35th-37th] stitch[es]. K to end of round.

Alternate decrease and non-decrease rounds until 62 [74] stitches remain. Repeat the non-decrease round until the sock reaches desired length before toe decreases. Stop after completing row 3 or 13 of the Main Chart. Note where you stop. Sock 1 and sock 2 will stop at opposite points.

Note, the toe decreases happen over 15 [16] rows. This will probably be something around 1.75 – 2 inches of length, but row gauge is notoriously variable, so I strongly suggest you actually measure how long that is on your socks. If you need to tweak the length bit, you can work the final row (row 3 or 13) an extra time or two to give yourself a bit of leeway.

TOE: The way you work the toes differs depending on whether you've stopped after row 3 or row 13 (you'll work one of each). Be sure to follow the appropriate directions.

If you stop after row 3:

Decrease round A: K until 3 stitches remain before first marker, k2tog, k1. Follow the appropriate Toe Chart to second marker. K to end of round. 2 stitches decreased.

Non-decrease round: K to first marker. Follow the appropriate Toe Chart to second marker. K to end of round.

Work these 2 rounds 2 times, 58 [70] stitches remain.

If you stop after row 13:

Decrease round A: K to first marker. Follow the appropriate Toe Chart to second marker. K1, ssk to end of round. 2 stitches decreased.

Non-decrease round: K to first marker. Follow the appropriate Toe Chart to second marker. K to end of round.

Work these 2 rounds 2 times, 58 [70] stitches remain.

For either sock:

Decrease round B: K until 3 stitches remain before first marker, k2tog, k1. Follow the appropriate Toe Chart to second marker. K1, ssk, k to end of round. 4 stitches decreased.

Work this round to end of appropriate Toe Chart, 14 [22] stitches remain. K to marker. Remove markers. Graft toes. Weave in ends.

NOTE: The shaded stitches are used to adjust sizing. Work the unshaded stitches for Small. Work all stitches for Large.

2X1 CABLE RIGHT PURL: Slip 1 to cn, hold in back, knit 2, purl 1 from cn.

2X2 CABLE RIGHT PURL: Slip 2 to cn, hold in back, knit 2, purl 2 from cn.

2X2 CABLE RIGHT: Slip 2 to cn, hold in back, knit 2, knit 2 from cn.

2X1 CABLE LEFT PURL: Slip 2 to cn, hold in front, purl 1, knit 2 from cn.

2X2 CABLE LEFT PURL: Slip 2 to cn, hold in front, purl 2, knit 2 from cn.

2X2 CABLE LEFT: Slip 2 to cn, hold in front, knit 2, knit 2 from cn.

KNIT FRONT, BACK, FRONT: Knit into the front, back, front of the same stitch.

Main Chart

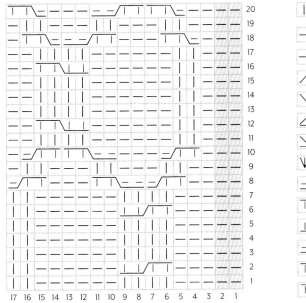

	RS: Knit WS: Purl
—	RS: Purl WS: Knit
→	Slip as if to purl
/	Knit 2 together
\	Slip slip knit
⟋	Purl 2 together
⟍	Slip slip purl
V	Knit into front, back, front
—⟋||	2x1 Cable right purl
||⟍—	2x1 Cable left purl
||⟋||	2x2 Cable right
— —⟋||	2x2 Cable right purl
||⟍||	2x2 Cable left
||⟍— —	2x2 Cable left purl

HEEL CHART (STOPPED AFTER ROW 10)

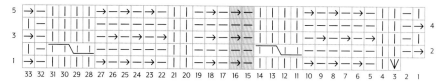

HEEL CHART (STOPPED AFTER ROW 20)

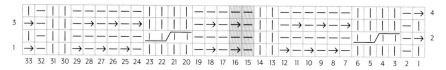

TOE CHART
SMALL (STOPPED
AFTER ROW 3)

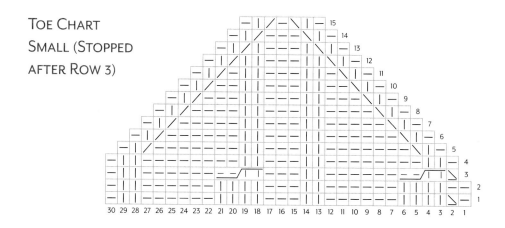

TOE CART
SMALL (STOPPED
AFTER ROW 13)

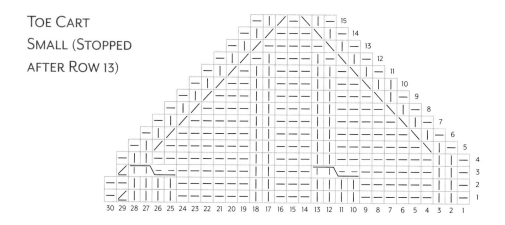

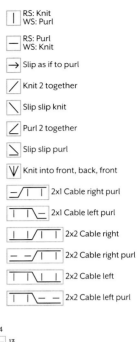

NOTE: The shaded stitches are used to adjust sizing. Work the unshaded stitches for Small. Work all stitches for Large.

	RS: Knit WS: Purl
	RS: Purl WS: Knit
→	Slip as if to purl
/	Knit 2 together
\	Slip slip knit
∠	Purl 2 together
⟍	Slip slip purl
V	Knit into front, back, front
	2x1 Cable right purl
	2x1 Cable left purl
	2x2 Cable right
	2x2 Cable right purl
	2x2 Cable left
	2x2 Cable left purl

TOE CHART LARGE (STOPPED AFTER ROW 3)

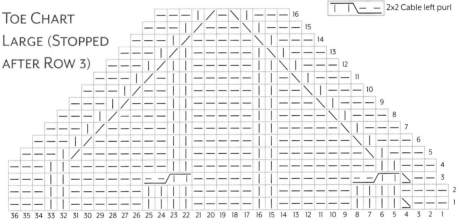

TOE CHART LARGE (STOPPED AFTER ROW 13)

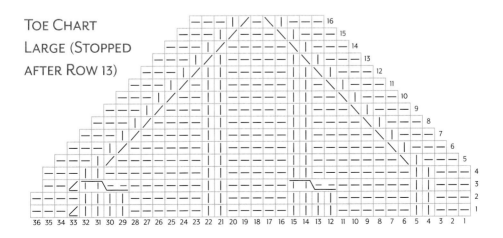

RUFFIAN

Shown in: Twist by Malabrigo in the colors Green Gray (color 1) and Indiecita (color 2). Made in size Medium with about 75 yards of each color (150 yards total) for each hat.

Gauge and Sizing: 14 sts in 4 inches in Main Chart stitch pattern. Fits a head of 20 [22.5, 25] inches.

Notes: The fabric relaxes dramatically with blocking. Be sure to measure gauge over a blocked swatch. The decreases happen quickly and will not give you any extra height. Be sure the hat is as tall as needed before starting them.

Hat A Main Chart

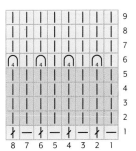

Hat A Decrease Chart

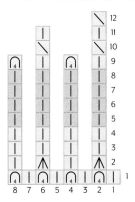

Hat A (shown opposite)

Cast on: With color 1, cast on 64 [72, 80] stitches. Place marker and join for working in the round.

Brim: Work row 1 of the Main Chart 8 times.

Body: Work rows 2-9 of the Main Chart until hat reaches desired height before the decreases. Stop after completing row 5 of the Main Chart.

Decreases: Work the Decrease Chart once. 8 [9, 10] stitches remain.

Finishing: Draw the yarn through remaining stitches. Weave in ends. Block.

	Knit
	Knit through the back loop
	Knit 4 below
—	Purl
\	Slip slip knit
∧	Centered double decrease
	Color 2
	Color 1

Knit 4 below: Insert your right needle into the stitch 4 stitches below the first stitch on your left needle. Wrap your yarn around the needle and pull it through, dropping the first stitch off your left needle.

Tug on the fabric to help the dropped stitch run down 4 stitches (the stitch you just made will catch it and keep your knitting from unraveling any farther).

Centered double decrease: Slip 2 together at the same time as if to knit 2 together. Knit 1. Pass the slipped stitches over.

HAT B (SHOWN OPPOSITE)

CAST ON: With color 1, cast on 64 [72, 80] stitches. Place marker and join for working in the round.

BRIM: Work row 1 of the Main Chart 8 times.

BODY: Work rows 2-11 of the Main Chart until hat reaches desired height before the decreases. Stop after completing row 6 of the Main Chart.

DECREASES: Work the Decrease Chart once. 8 [9, 10] stitches remain.

FINISHING: Draw the yarn through remaining stitches. Weave in ends. Block if desired.

HAT B MAIN CHART

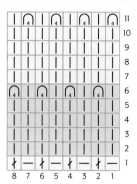

KNIT 4 BELOW: Insert your right needle into the stitch 4 stitches below the first stitch on your left needle. Wrap your yarn around the needle and pull it through, dropping the first stitch off your left needle.

Tug on the fabric to help the dropped stitch run down 4 stitches (the stitch you just made will catch it and keep your knitting from unraveling any farther).

CENTERED DOUBLE DECREASE: Slip 2 together at the same time as if to knit 2 together. Knit 1. Pass the slipped stitches over.

HAT B DECREASE CHART

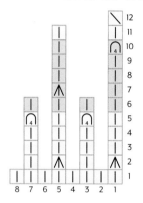

|	Knit
⸕	Knit through the back loop
⋒₄	Knit 4 below
—	Purl
╲	Slip slip knit
⋀	Centered double decrease
▨	Color 2
☐	Color 1

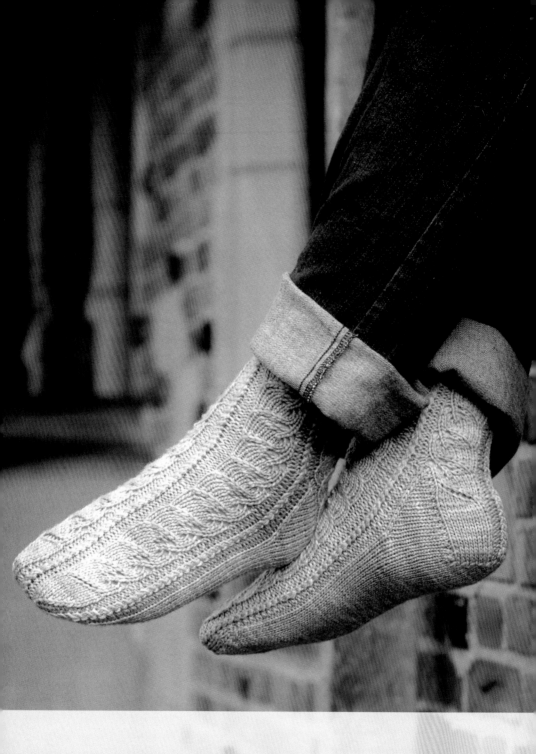

VANDAL

SHOWN IN: Chubbie by Vice in the color Blue Stone. Made in size Large with about 270 yards of yarn.

GAUGE AND SIZING: 26 stitches in 4 inches in stockinette. Fits a foot or leg of about 8.5 [9.5] inches.

CAST ON: Cast on 48 [56] stitches. Place marker and join for working in the round.

CUFF AND LEG: Work the appropriate Main Chart until sock reaches desired height. Stop after completing row 8 of the appropriate Main Chart.

HEEL FLAP: The heel flap is worked over stitches 27-48 [31-56]. It uses 22 [26] stitches. Row 1 is a wrong-side row (worked with the inside of the sock facing you). Row 2 is a right side-row (worked with the outside of the sock facing you). Work the appropriate Heel Chart once. Repeat rows 17 and 18 of the appropriate Heel Chart until heel reaches desired length.

HEEL TURN: Odd rows are wrong-side rows (worked with the inside of the sock facing you following the wrong-side notations in the stitch key, and reading the chart from left to right). Even rows are right-side rows (worked with the outside of the sock facing you, following the right-side notations in the stitch key, and reading the chart from right to left). Turn at the end of each row.

Row 1 (WS): Sl1, p12 [14], p2tog, p1.
Row 2 (RS): Sl1, k5 [5], ssk, k1.
Row 3 (WS): Sl1, p to 1 stitch before gap, p2tog, p1.
Row 4 (RS): Sl1, knit to 1 stitch before gap, ssk, k1.

Work rows 3 and 4 until 14 [16] stitches remain.

GUSSET AND FOOT: Pick up and knit stitches along the side of the heel flap,

place first marker. Work across the top of the foot following the appropriate Main Chart (work 2 full repeats of the Main Chart and then work the first 2 stitches again), place second marker. Pick up and knit stitches along the other side of the heel flap, k7 [8]. The round now begins in the middle of the bottom of the foot.

Decrease round: K until 3 [4] stitches remain before first marker, k2tog, p1 [2]. Work across the top of the foot following the next row of the appropriate Main Chart (work 2 full repeats of the Main Chart and then work the first 2 stitches again). P1 [2], ssk, k to end of round. 2 stitches decreased.

Non-decrease round: K until 1 [2] stitches remain before first marker, p1 [2]. Work across the top of the foot following the next row of the appropriate Chart (work 2 full repeats of the Main Chart and then work the first 2 stitches again). P1 [2], k to end of round.

Alternate decrease and non-decrease rounds until 52 [60] stitches remain (count on an odd row).

Repeat the non-decrease round until 3.5 inches shorter than desired length. Stop after completing row 8 of the appropriate Main Chart. Work the appropriate Toe Chart once. Repeat rows 8 and 9 of the appropriate Toe Chart until sock measures 1.75 [2] inches shorter than desired length.

TOE: Decrease round: K until 3 [4] stitches remain before first marker, k2tog, k1 [2]. Work 2 stitches as established, p1[2], ssk, follow pattern as established until 5 [6] stitches remain before second marker, k2tog, p1 [2], work 2 stitches as established. K1 [2], ssk, k to end of round. 4 stitches decreased.

Non-decrease round: K to first marker. P1 [2], follow pattern as established until 1

[2] stitches remain before second marker, p1 [2]. K to end of round.

Work these 2 rounds 4 [6] times, 36 stitches remain. Work the decrease round 4 more times, 20 stitches remain. K to marker. Remove markers. Graft toes. Weave in ends.

	RS:Knit WS: Purl
—	RS: Purl WS: Knit
→	Slip as if to purl
O	Yarn over
⌐	RS: Make 1 right WS: Make 1 right purlwise
⌐	RS: Make 1 left WS: Make 1 left purlwise
/	RS: Knit 2 together WS: Purl 2 together
\	RS: Slip slip knit WS: Slip slip purl through the back loop
⊥/⊤	Right twist
⊤\⊥	Left twist
▒	No stitch

RIGHT TWIST: Slip 1 to cn, hold in back, k1tbl, k1tbl from cn.

LEFT TWIST: Slip 1 to cn, hold in front, k1tbl, k1tbl from cn.

MAKE 1 RIGHT: With left needle, lift strand of yarn between stitches from back to front. Knit into the loop thus created.

MAKE 1 LEFT: With left needle, lift strand of yarn between stitches from front to back. Knit into the back of the loop thus created.

MAKE 1 RIGHT PURLWISE: With left needle, lift strand of yarn between stitches from back to front. Purl into the loop thus created.

MAKE 1 LEFT PURLWISE: With left needle, lift strand of yarn between stitches from front to back. Purl into the back of the loop thus created.

LEFT MAIN CHART

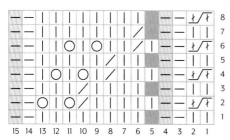

RIGHT MAIN CHART

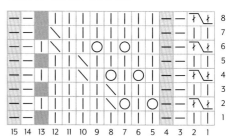

LEFT TOE CHART

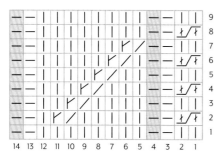

RIGHT TOE CHART

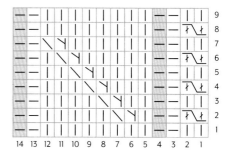

Left Heel Chart

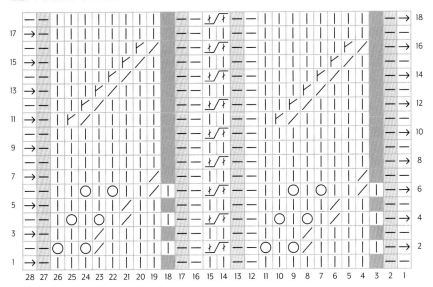

Right Heel Chart

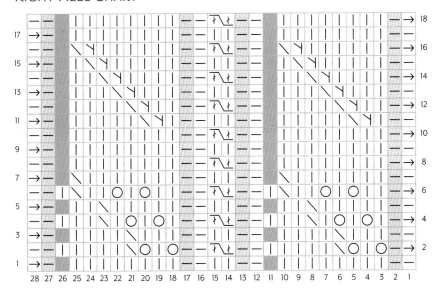

NOTE: The shaded stitches are used to adjust sizing. Work the unshaded stitches for Small. Work all stitches for Large.

BRIGAND

Shown in: Tibetan Dream by Bijou Spun in the color Sky. Made in size Small with about 160 yards of yarn.

Gauge and sizing: At 6.5 stitches per inch in Main Chart stitch pattern, fits an arm of about 7.5 [9.25] inches. At 7 stitches per inch, fits an arm of about 7 [8.5] inches. At 7.5 stitches per inch, fits an arm of about 6.5 [8] inches. Measure at the widest part of the forearm that you want the mitt to cover. Shown at 6.5 stitches per inch.

Note: To make the mitts mirror each other, you must start and stop following the Main Chart at different points for the left and right mitt. Pay close attention to the instructions.

Cast on: Cast on 44 [55] stitches. Place marker and join for working in the round.

Setup: Work row 1 of the Main Chart 2 times

Wrist: For the Left mitt, work the Main Chart until wrist reaches desired length (measured to the base of the palm). Stop after completing row 4 of the Main Chart.

For the Right mitt, start following the Main Chart at row 3. Work the Main Chart until wrist reaches desired length (measured to the base of the palm). Stop after completing row 2 of the Main Chart.

Thumb: to make the thumb, you will gradually create 13 [15] extra stitches. These stitches will appear between the 2 purl stitches that start the round.

To do this, locate the first stitch of the round. Place 2 stitch markers between it and the second stitch of the round. Work the next row of the Thumb Chart between these two stitches. Work the rest of the round in pattern as established. Work through 13 [15] rows of the Thumb Chart

in this fashion. You will have a total of 57 [70] stitches.

Hand, part 1: Work in pattern as established (working the thumb in knit 1 through the back loop, purl 1 ribbing) until the glove is tall enough to reach the middle of your palm. For the Right mitt, stop after completing row 4 of the Main Chart. For the Left mitt, stop after completing row 2 of the Main Chart.

Hand, part 2: Remove the stitch markers used to mark off the 13 [15] stitches you created for the thumb gusset and set these stitches aside on a spare needle or length of scrap yarn. The 2 purl stitches that start the round are now next to each other again. Work the Main Chart until mitt reaches the base of your fingers. For the Right mitt, stop after completing row 4 of the Main Chart. For the Left mitt, stop after completing row 2 of the Main Chart. Work row 1 of the Main Chart 2 times. Cast off loosely.

Thumb: Divide the 13 [15] stitches set aside for the thumb across two needles. Pick up 3 [5] stitches to bridge the gap between the first and last of the set aside thumb stitches. You will have 16 [20] thumb stitches. Work in knit 1 through the back loop, purl 1 ribbing as established until thumb reaches desired length.

Finishing: Cast off loosely. Weave in ends. Block if desired.

Main Chart

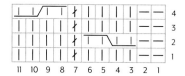

I	Knit
≀	Knit through the back loop
—	Purl
◯	Yarn over
2x2 Cable right	2x2 Cable right
2x2 Cable left	2x2 Cable left

Left Thumb Chart

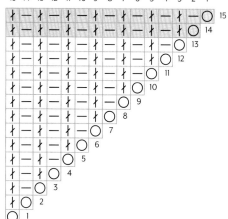

Right Thumb Chart

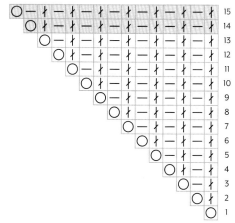

NOTE: The Left and Right mitts use different charts. Be sure to follow the appropriate chart. The shaded stitches are used to adjust sizing. Work the unshaded stitches for Small. Work all stitches for Large.

2X2 CABLE RIGHT: Slip 2 to cn, hold in back, knit 2, knit 2 from cn.

2X2 CABLE LEFT: Slip 2 to cn, hold in front, knit 2, knit 2 from cn.

SABOTEUR

SHOWN IN: Casbah by Handmaiden in the color Peridot. Made in size Small with about 300 yards of yarn.

GAUGE AND SIZING: 9 stitches in 1 inch in stockinette. Fits a foot or leg of 8.5 [9.5] inches.

NOTE: The lace fabric is quite open and so requires fewer stitches to produce a given width of fabric. This explains the slightly lower than average stitch count in the leg.

CAST ON: Cast on 56 [64] stitches. Place marker and join for working in the round.

CUFF AND LEG: Work row 1 of the appropriate Chart 8 [7] times. For the Large only, work row 2 of the Large Chart 1 time. 0 [4] stitches increased.

Work rows 2-17 [3-20] of the appropriate Chart once.

Work rows 18-33 [21-40] of the appropriate Chart until sock reaches desired height. Stop after completing row 33 [40] of the appropriate Chart.

HEEL FLAP: The heel flap is worked over stitches 30-56 [36-68]. It uses 27 [33] stitches. Row 1 is a wrong-side row (worked with the inside of the sock facing you). Row 2 is a right side-row (worked with the outside of the sock facing you). Work these 2 rows 15 [17] times or until heel flap reaches desired length.

Row 1 (WS): (Sl1, p1) 13 [16] times, k1.
Row 2 (RS): Sl1, (k1, p1) 13 [16] times.

HEEL TURN: Odd rows are wrong-side rows (worked with the inside of the sock facing you). Even rows are right-side rows (worked with the outside of the sock facing you). Turn at the end of each row.

Row 1 (WS): Sl1, p15 [17], p2tog, p1.
Row 2 (RS): Sl1, k6 [4], ssk, k1.

Row 3 (WS): Sl1, p to 1 stitch before gap, p2tog, p1.
Row 4 (RS): Sl1, knit to 1 stitch before gap, ssk, k1.

Work rows 3 and 4 until 17 [19] stitches remain.

GUSSET AND FOOT: Pick up and knit stitches along the side of the heel flap, place first marker. Work across the top of the foot following row 18 [21] of the appropriate Chart for the first 28 [34] stitches, p the 29th [35th] stitch, place second marker. Pick up and knit stitches along the other side of the heel flap, k8 [9]. The round now begins in the middle of the bottom of the foot.

Decrease round: K until 3 stitches remain before first marker, k2tog, k1. Work across the top of the foot following the next row of the appropriate Chart for the first 28 [34] stitches, p the 29th [35th] stitch. K1, ssk, k to end of round. 2 stitches decreased.

Non-decrease round: K to first marker. Work across the top of the foot following the next row of the appropriate Chart for the first 28 [34] stitches, p the 29th [35th] stitch. K to end of round.

Alternate decrease and non-decrease rounds while repeating rows 18-33 [21-40] of the appropriate Chart until 58 [70] stitches remain.

Repeat the non-decrease round until you have worked 2 repeats of rows 18-33 [21-40] of the appropriate Chart (if you want the pattern to extend farther down the foot, work thes rows 1 more time). The last time you work row 32 [39] of the appropriate Chart, do not work stitches 2, 3, 27, and 28 [2, 3, 33, and 34] of that row as written on the Chart. Instead, work these 4 stitches as plain knit stitches. Stop after completing row 33 [40] of the appropriate Chart.

Work rows 34-51 [41-62] of the appropriate Chart once. Continue to p the 29th [35th] stitch of the round. Repeat row 51 [62] of the appropriate Chart until sock measures 2 [2.5] inches shorter than desired length.

TOE: Decrease round: K until 3 stitches remain before first marker, k2tog, k1. P1, ssk, k until 3 stitches remain before second marker, k2tog, p1. K1, ssk, k to end of round. 4 stitches decreased.

Non-decrease round: K to first marker. P1, k until 1 stitch remains before second marker, p1. K to end of round.

Work these 2 rounds 4 [7] times, 42 stitches remain. Work the decrease round 6 more times, 18 stitches remain. K to marker. Remove markers. Graft toes. Weave in ends.

NOTES: The red lines on the charts indicate the different sections mentioned in the instructions. The sizes use different charts. Be sure to follow the appropriate chart.

RIGHT-LEANING DECREASE, TWISTED: Slip 1 knitwise. Slip another 1 knitwise. Return slipped stitches to the left needle. Knit 2 together.

LEFT-LEANING DECREASE, TWISTED: Insert the right needle from the right to the left into the backloops of 2 stitches. Knit them together.

CENTERED DOUBLE DECREASE: Slip 2 together at the same time as if to knit 2 together. Knit 1. Pass the slipped stitches over.

CENTERED DOUBLE DECREASE, TWISTED: Slip 1 as if to purl. Remount next stitch so it is rotated 180 degrees clockwise. Slip the first stitch back onto the left needle. Slip 2 together at the same time as if to knit 2 together. Knit 1. Pass slipped stitches over.

SMALL CHART

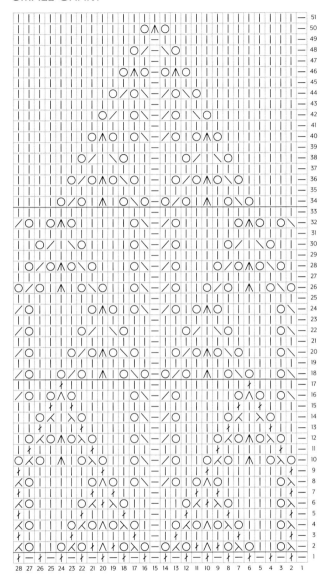

I	Knit
ʄ	Knit through the back loop
—	Purl
O	Yarn over
/	Right-leaning decrease (k2tog)
⟋	Right-leaning decrease, twisted
\	Left-leaning decrease (ssk)
⟍	Left-leaning decrease, twisted
⋀	Centered double decrease
⋀	Centered double decrease, twisted

LARGE CHART

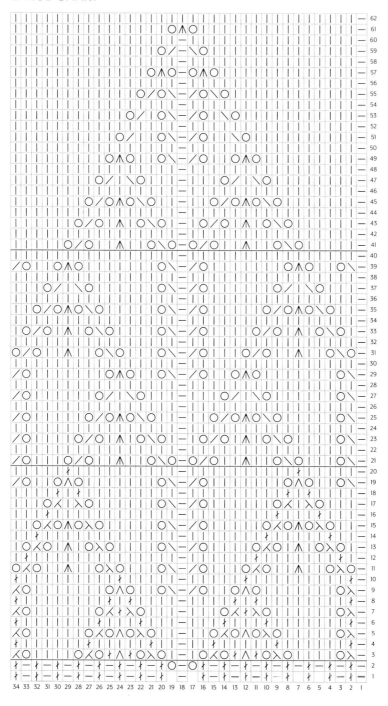

TIPS & TRICKS

ABBREVIATIONS: k-knit, p-purl, k2tog-knit 2 together, p2tog-purl 2 together, cn-cable needle, RS-right or public side, WS-wrong or private side.

CAST ON: Use your favorite stretchy cast on; shown with the long-tailed cast on.

CAST OFF: Use your favorite stretchy cast off. Jeny's Surprisingly Stretchy Bind Off is a good choice.

CHART NOTES: Some charts include notes to highlight particular features or help you with potential trouble spots. Read them carefully before you begin.

NEEDLES: These patterns work with any style of needle. You may notice that needle sizes are not listed. This is because *every knitter knits differently*, and the needles you need to get gauge are likely different than the needles another knitter needs to get gauge. The best and most accurate way to get gauge is always to swatch.

NOTES: Several of the patterns include special notes to draw your attention to important aspects of the pattern. Read them carefully before you begin.

SIZING: Each of the patterns is offered in at least two sizes. Sometimes stitch counts or pattern repeats differ from one size to the next. This is indicated by first giving the stitch count or pattern repeat for the smallest size and then giving the stitch count or pattern repeat for the larger sizes in square brackets. If there is more than one larger size, the stitch counts or pattern repeats in square brackets will be separated by commas.

SLIPPED STITCHES: Many of the projects call for slipping stitches along the edge of the knitting to create a tidy selvage edge. There are almost as many ways to do this as there are knitters. As long as you are getting elongated stitches along the edge of the fabric, you're doing it right!

One approach that works for most people is to always slip the first stitch as if to purl with your yarn held to the wrong side of the fabric. If you find that's not working for the way you knit, you can also try holding the yarn to the back of the work and slipping as if to knit on right-side rows and holding the yarn to the front of the work and slipping as if to purl on wrong-side rows.

STITCH MARKERS: Most patterns suggest using a stitch marker to indicate the beginning of the round. This is optional, but it can make it easier to see what you're doing. If you find them helpful, you may also wish to use stitch markers to separate pattern repeats.

SWATCHES: Swatches will save you a huge amount of time in the long run. They are a good idea, even on simple projects. Be sure to swatch in the stitch pattern listed in the gauge and sizing section. Always block your swatch before measuring.

YARN REQUIREMENTS: Each pattern lists a generous estimate for the yarn needed to complete the project. This is a good guideline, but estimating yardage requirements is a bit of a black art. If you decide to make your socks knee highs, or to make your fingerless gloves elbow length, you're going to need more yarn. When in doubt, buy extra! It's much easier to return an unneeded skein than to run out on the last row.

THANKS

I don't know if you can tell, but I'm having a ridiculously good time with these mini books. They're a perfect project, big enough to sink my teeth into but not so big as to be daunting. I love making them, and I want to start by thanking all of you who have made room for them on your shelves for letting me have so much fun!

Many thanks are also due to my marvelous test knitters. They find my mistakes so you don't have to. The brave souls who helped with this project are: Kathleen Welch, Marion Schling, Raylene Funk, Katie Metzroth, Deb Jaworowicz, Suzanne Sunday, Jen Speer, Barb Stephenson, Lila Guterman, Audrey Tam, Sara Varty, Sabine Konrath, Jessica Powers, Yvonne Spencer, Lisa Beth Houchins, Kristi Renshaw, Georgina Allison, and a few super-secret helpers who prefer to remain anonymous.

Cathy Scott (creator of the marvelous StitchMastery charting software) and Heather Ordover (mastermind behind the Craftlit empire) are my amazing editors, and they deserve both my thanks and yours. Cathy makes sure I don't lead you astray in the patterns, and Heather makes sure I don't embarrass myself by abusing the English language in public.

I must also thank the charming Laura Lazarites for saying yes when I asked her if she'd like to spend an afternoon driving around the sketchier parts of town taking pictures. My tremendously accommodating husband Brian also said yes to a host of similar requests (including one for a sunrise trip to the railroad tracks). For this, and for the countless other ways in which he supports this crazy undertaking of mine, I am forever grateful.

Cat Bordhi's Visionary Authors group is a marvelous resource for designers who want to publish their own books. Being able to talk with other people who understand the process is hugely helpful, and I'm thrilled (and just a little surprised) that they let me in their clubhouse.

And last but not least, many thanks to my family. They've taken this odd career choice of mine in stride and fully support my plans for woolly world domination.

RESOURCES

MISCREANT uses about half of a 230-yard skein of Astrid by Space Cadet Creations.

SCOUNDREL uses two 280-yard skeins of Merino DK by String Theory. If you were making very small socks, you might squeak by with one skein.

DESPERADO uses about 75 yards of each of two colors of Twist by Malabrigo for each hat. Both hats were made from a 150-yard skein of each color.

VANDAL uses nearly all of a 274-yard skein of Chubbie by Vice. If you're making size 9 or above, you may need two skeins.

BRIGAND uses less than half of a 440-yard skein of Tibetan Dream by Bijou Spun.

SABOTEUR uses almost all of a 350-yard skein of Casbah by Handmaiden.

CHARTS were created with StitchMastery Knitting Chart Editor.